THE AUTONOM FUTURE

FUTURE

MASTERING AGENTIC AI

OLIVER LUCAS JR

Preface

The age of artificial intelligence is upon us, and with it, a new era of autonomy. We stand at the cusp of a technological revolution, where intelligent agents, capable of independent thought and action, are poised to reshape our world. This book, "The Autonomous Future: Mastering Agentic AI," is your guide to understanding and navigating this transformative landscape.

For decades, artificial intelligence has been largely confined to the realm of reactive systems, responding to inputs with pre-programmed rules. But the emergence of agentic AI marks a paradigm shift, moving beyond passive responses to proactive, goal-oriented behavior. These intelligent agents, driven by principles of autonomy, learning, and interaction, are not merely tools; they are collaborators, problem-solvers, and potential architects of our future.

This book is not just a theoretical exploration; it's a practical roadmap. We will delve into the core principles of agentic AI, explore the architectures and frameworks that underpin these systems, and examine the ethical considerations that must guide their development. From the intricacies of reinforcement learning and self-supervised learning to the challenges of ensuring fairness and transparency, we will navigate the complexities of this evolving field.

We will also explore the real-world applications of agentic AI, from autonomous robotics and intelligent personal assistants to its transformative impact on healthcare, finance, and education. We will examine the crucial role of natural language processing in enabling seamless human-agent communication, and we will confront the profound questions surrounding machine consciousness and the future of human-agent collaboration.

As you embark on this journey, you will gain the knowledge and insights needed to understand, build, and deploy agentic AI systems. Whether you are a seasoned AI researcher, a budding developer, or simply a curious observer, this book will equip you with the tools to master the autonomous future.

The potential of agentic AI is vast, but its responsible development is paramount. By understanding the principles, mastering the techniques, and embracing the ethical considerations, we can ensure that this powerful technology serves humanity and shapes a future where intelligence and autonomy work in harmony.

Welcome to the autonomous future.

TABLE OF CONTENTS

Chapter 5

Chapter 6

Chapter 7

Chapter 8

Chapter 9

9.1 Exploring Cognitive Architectures: Human-Inspired AI

9.2 The Debate on Machine Consciousness and Sentience

9.3 Future Directions: Integrating Neuroscience and AI

Chapter 10

10.1 Step-by-Step Implementation: From Concept to Deployment

10.2 Tools and Resources: Libraries, APIs, and Datasets

10.3 Best Practices and Future Trends in Agentic AI Development

Chapter 1

The Dawn of Agentic AI

1.1 Defining Agentic AI: Beyond Traditional Algorithms

1.1.1 From Reactive to Proactive: The Shift in AI Paradigm

Traditional artificial intelligence has often been characterized by its reactive nature. Systems are designed to respond to specific inputs, executing pre-programmed rules or applying learned patterns. A thermostat, for example, reacts to temperature changes by turning the heating or cooling system on or off. While effective in controlled environments, this approach lacks the adaptability and initiative required for truly intelligent behavior. Agentic AI represents a fundamental shift towards proactive systems. Instead of merely reacting, these agents initiate actions, pursue goals, and generate their own strategies. Consider a smart home system powered by agentic AI. It doesn't just respond to temperature fluctuations; it anticipates them, learns your preferences, and optimizes energy usage proactively. This capability to move beyond passive responses is a hallmark of agentic systems, enabling them to navigate complex and dynamic environments with greater autonomy.

1.1.2 The Essence of "Agency": Intentionality and Autonomy

At the core of agentic AI lies the concept of "agency." This refers to the capacity of an AI system to act independently and make choices with a degree of intentionality. It's more than just executing commands; it involves setting goals, planning actions, and making decisions based on perceived information and internal reasoning. While the philosophical debate on whether AI can truly possess "intentionality" continues, the practical implementation of agency translates to systems that can autonomously adapt to changing circumstances. Autonomy, in this context, exists on a spectrum. A robot following a fixed set of instructions has minimal autonomy, whereas an agent that can dynamically adjust its actions based on real-time feedback and evolving goals exhibits a higher degree of agency. This capacity for self-directed action is what distinguishes agentic AI from its more passive predecessors.

1.1.3 Cognitive Loops: Perception, Reasoning, and Action in Agentic Systems

Agentic AI operates through continuous cognitive loops, comprising perception, reasoning, and action. Perception involves gathering information from the environment through sensors or data inputs. Reasoning entails processing that information, understanding the situation, and formulating strategies. Action is the execution of those strategies, influencing the environment. These cognitive loops are supported by memory and knowledge representation, allowing agents to learn from past experiences and apply that knowledge to new situations. Feedback loops play a critical role, enabling agents to evaluate their performance and refine their strategies over time. For instance, an autonomous vehicle uses sensors to perceive its surroundings, reasons about the traffic conditions and potential hazards, and then takes actions like steering and braking. These cognitive loops are not isolated processes; they interact and influence each other, enabling the emergence of complex and adaptive behaviors

1.2 The Evolution: From Rule-Based Systems to Autonomous Agents

1.2.1 The Era of Rule-Based Systems: Defining Early AI

The earliest forms of artificial intelligence were largely defined by rule-based systems. These systems operated on a set of pre-defined rules, where specific inputs triggered corresponding outputs. This approach was effective for tasks with clearly defined parameters, such as simple decision-making or basic pattern recognition. Expert systems, for example, encoded human knowledge into a set of rules to solve problems in specific domains. However, these systems were inherently limited by their rigidity. They struggled to adapt to novel situations or handle ambiguous data, as they lacked the capacity for learning or independent reasoning. The "if-then" logic that characterized rule-based systems, while foundational, represented a constrained form of intelligence.

1.2.2 The Rise of Machine Learning: Statistical Patterns and Adaptability

The emergence of machine learning marked a significant step towards more adaptive AI. By enabling systems to learn from data, machine learning introduced the ability to recognize patterns and make predictions without explicit programming. Algorithms like neural networks and support vector machines allowed AI to handle more complex tasks, such as image recognition and natural language processing. This shift from rule-based to data-driven approaches brought greater flexibility and adaptability. However, even with machine learning, AI systems remained largely passive, responding to inputs based on learned patterns rather than actively pursuing goals. The focus was on prediction and classification, rather than autonomous action and strategic planning.

1.2.3 The Emergence of Agentic AI: Towards True Autonomy

Agentic AI represents the culmination of this evolutionary trajectory, moving beyond passive learning to active autonomy. This paradigm shift is characterized by the integration of cognitive capabilities, such as perception, reasoning, and planning, into AI systems. Agentic agents are not merely reactive; they are proactive, capable of setting goals, making independent decisions, and adapting to dynamic environments. This evolution is driven by advancements in areas like reinforcement learning, cognitive architectures, and multi-agent systems, which enable the development of AI that can operate with greater independence and intelligence. The transition from rule-based systems to machine learning and finally to agentic AI reflects a continuous pursuit of creating AI that can not only process information but also act intelligently and autonomously in the world.

1.3 The Core Principles: Autonomy, Learning, and Interaction

1.3.1 Autonomy: Independent Decision-Making and Action

Autonomy is the cornerstone of agentic AI. It signifies the ability of an agent to make independent decisions and take actions without constant external control. This goes beyond simply following pre-programmed instructions; it involves the capacity to assess situations, evaluate options, and choose the most appropriate course of action. True autonomy requires agents to possess a degree of self-sufficiency, enabling them to operate effectively in dynamic and unpredictable environments. This includes the ability to set goals, plan strategies, and execute tasks without continuous human intervention. The level of autonomy can vary, but the fundamental principle remains: agentic systems must be capable of independent operation to achieve their objectives.

1.3.2 Learning: Continuous Adaptation and Knowledge Acquisition

Learning is another essential principle that distinguishes agentic AI. These systems are not static; they continuously adapt and improve their performance through experience. This involves acquiring new knowledge, refining existing strategies, and adjusting to changing circumstances. Learning in agentic AI can take various forms, including reinforcement learning, where agents learn through trial and error; self-supervised learning, where agents learn from unlabeled data; and transfer learning, where agents apply knowledge gained from one task to another. This capacity for continuous learning enables agentic systems to handle complex and evolving situations, making them more robust and adaptable than traditional AI.

1.3.3 Interaction: Engaging with the Environment and Other Agents

Interaction is the third core principle, highlighting the importance of agentic systems' ability to engage with their environment and other agents. This involves perceiving and interpreting information from the surrounding world, as well as communicating and collaborating with other entities. Effective interaction requires agents to possess sophisticated communication protocols, the ability to understand and respond to diverse stimuli, and the capacity to coordinate actions with other agents. This principle is particularly crucial in multi-agent systems, where agents must work together to achieve common goals. Interaction also extends to human-agent collaboration, requiring agents to understand and respond to human needs and preferences. By effectively interacting with their environment and other agents, agentic systems can navigate complex social and physical landscapes, enabling them to achieve their objectives in a collaborative and coordinated manner.

Chapter 2

Architectures and Frameworks for Agentic Systems

2.1 Designing Cognitive Architectures: Planning, Reasoning, and Execution

2.1.1 The Blueprint of Intelligence: Defining Cognitive Architectures

Cognitive architectures provide the foundational blueprint for agentic AI, defining the structure and processes that enable intelligent behavior.[1] They serve as the framework within which planning, reasoning, and execution occur.[2] A cognitive architecture is more than just a collection of algorithms; it's a unified system that integrates various cognitive functions, such as perception, memory, reasoning, and action.[3] These architectures aim to emulate the cognitive processes of intelligent beings, providing a structured approach to building autonomous agents.[4] Key considerations in designing cognitive architectures include the representation of knowledge, the flow of information, and the mechanisms for decision-making. The goal is to create a cohesive system that can effectively manage complexity and achieve desired outcomes.

2.1.2 Strategic Thinking: Planning and Goal-Oriented Behavior

Planning is a critical component of cognitive architectures, enabling agents to formulate strategies and achieve their goals.[5] This involves anticipating future events, evaluating potential actions, and selecting the most effective course of action. Effective planning requires agents to have a clear understanding of their goals, the ability to model their environment, and the capacity to reason about the consequences of their actions. Planning algorithms, such as hierarchical task networks and reinforcement learning-based planners, play a crucial role in enabling agents to generate and execute complex plans.[6] Goal-oriented behavior is the outcome of effective planning, ensuring that agents act purposefully and strategically.

2.1.3 From Thought to Action: Reasoning and Execution Mechanisms

Reasoning and execution are the mechanisms that translate plans into concrete actions. Reasoning involves processing information, drawing inferences, and making decisions based on available knowledge.[7] This can include deductive reasoning, inductive reasoning, and abductive reasoning, depending on the nature of the task. Execution involves the physical or virtual implementation of planned actions, influencing the agent's environment.[8] Cognitive architectures must provide efficient and reliable mechanisms for both reasoning and execution to ensure that agents can effectively achieve their goals. This includes the ability to handle uncertainty, adapt to changing circumstances, and learn from experience.[9]The seamless integration of reasoning and execution is essential for creating robust and adaptable agentic systems.

2.2 Frameworks and Platforms: Building and Deploying Agentic AI

2.2.1 The Developer's Toolkit: Software Frameworks for Agentic Systems

Building agentic AI requires robust software frameworks that provide the necessary tools and libraries for development. These frameworks abstract away the complexities of low-level implementation, allowing developers to focus on designing and implementing agent behavior. Frameworks like TensorFlow Agents, RLlib, and OpenAI Gym offer pre-built components for reinforcement learning, cognitive architectures, and multi-agent systems. They provide libraries for defining agent behavior, simulating environments, and training models. Additionally, frameworks like ROS (Robot Operating System) provide tools for building robotic agents and integrating them with physical environments. These frameworks often include support for various programming languages and offer modular architectures, enabling developers to customize and extend their functionalities. By leveraging these powerful tools, developers can accelerate the development process and build sophisticated agentic systems.

2.2.2 The Infrastructure Backbone: Cloud Platforms and Scalable Deployment

Deploying agentic AI systems often requires significant computational resources and scalable infrastructure. Cloud platforms like Amazon Web Services (AWS), Google Cloud Platform (GCP), and Microsoft Azure provide the necessary infrastructure for training and deploying agentic models. These platforms offer virtual machines, containerization services, and serverless computing, enabling developers to scale their applications as needed. Cloud platforms also provide access to pre-trained models, data storage, and machine learning services, facilitating the development and deployment of agentic AI. Furthermore, edge computing platforms enable the deployment of agentic systems on devices closer to the data source, reducing latency and improving real-time performance. This infrastructure backbone is essential for building and deploying agentic AI systems that can handle complex tasks and large-scale deployments.

2.2.3 Orchestrating Agentic Ecosystems: Multi-Agent Platforms and Simulation Environments

Multi-agent systems require platforms that can orchestrate the interactions and behaviors of multiple agents. Simulation environments play a crucial role in developing and testing multi-agent systems before deploying them in real-world scenarios. Platforms like Mesa, NetLogo, and Unity ML-Agents provide tools for creating and simulating multi-agent environments. These platforms allow developers to define agent behaviors, simulate interactions, and analyze emergent behaviors. They also offer features for visualizing agent interactions and collecting data for analysis. Additionally, platforms like Kubernetes can be used to manage and deploy large-scale multi-agent systems in distributed environments. These platforms provide the necessary tools for coordinating agent interactions, managing resources, and ensuring system reliability. By leveraging these platforms and simulation environments, developers can build and deploy complex agentic ecosystems that can tackle real-world problems.

Alright, let's craft section 2.3, "The Role of Memory and Knowledge Representation," focusing on how agents store and utilize information.

2.3 The Role of Memory and Knowledge Representation

2.3.1 Building the Agent's Mind: Memory Architectures for Agentic Systems

Memory is fundamental to intelligent behavior, enabling agents to learn from past experiences and apply that knowledge to future situations.[1] In agentic AI, memory architectures play a crucial role in storing and retrieving information.[2] Different types of memory are used, including short-term memory, long-term memory, and episodic memory.[3] Short-term memory, or working memory, allows agents to hold and manipulate information temporarily, enabling them to perform tasks that require immediate processing.[4] Long-term memory stores information over extended periods, providing agents with a repository of knowledge and experiences.[5] Episodic memory stores specific events and experiences, allowing agents to recall and learn from past situations.[6] Memory architectures can be implemented using various techniques, such as neural networks, graph databases, and symbolic representations. The design of memory architectures is critical for enabling agents to learn, adapt, and make informed decisions.[7]

2.3.2 Encoding Understanding: Knowledge Representation Techniques

Knowledge representation is the process of encoding information in a format that can be understood and used by agentic systems.[8] This involves defining the concepts, relationships, and rules that constitute the agent's knowledge base. Various knowledge representation techniques are used, including symbolic representations, such as ontologies and knowledge graphs; neural representations, such as embeddings and neural networks; and hybrid representations, which combine symbolic and neural approaches.[9] Ontologies provide a structured vocabulary and set of relationships for representing knowledge in a domain.[10] Knowledge graphs represent knowledge as a network of entities and relationships.[11] Neural embeddings represent concepts as vectors in a high-dimensional space, capturing semantic relationships.[12] The choice of knowledge representation technique depends on the nature of the task and the type of knowledge being represented. Effective knowledge representation enables agents to reason, plan, and make informed decisions based on their understanding of the world.[13]

2.3.3 Accessing and Utilizing Information: Knowledge Retrieval and Reasoning

Knowledge retrieval and reasoning are the processes by which agents access and utilize stored information to solve problems and make decisions.[14] Knowledge retrieval involves searching and retrieving relevant information from memory or knowledge bases.[15] Reasoning involves applying logical rules and inference mechanisms to derive new knowledge from existing information.[16] Techniques for knowledge retrieval include semantic search, graph traversal, and neural retrieval. Reasoning techniques include deductive reasoning, inductive reasoning, and abductive reasoning.[17]Deductive reasoning involves deriving conclusions from premises using logical rules.[18] Inductive reasoning involves generalizing from specific examples to general principles.[19] Abductive reasoning involves generating explanations for observed phenomena.[20] By effectively retrieving and reasoning with knowledge, agents can solve complex problems, make informed decisions, and adapt to changing circumstances.[21]

Chapter 3

Learning and Adaptation in Autonomous Agents

3.1 Reinforcement Learning for Agentic Behavior

3.1.1 Learning Through Interaction: The Principles of Reinforcement Learning

Reinforcement learning (RL) provides a powerful framework for enabling agentic behavior by allowing agents to learn through interaction with their environment. Unlike supervised learning, which relies on labeled data, RL focuses on learning from rewards and penalties. An agent operating within an environment takes actions, observes the outcomes, and receives feedback in the form of rewards or punishments. The agent's goal is to maximize the cumulative reward over time. This process of trial and error allows the agent to discover optimal strategies for achieving its objectives. Key components of RL include the agent, the environment, the state, the action, and the reward. The agent learns a policy, which maps states to actions, by iteratively updating its understanding of the environment and the consequences of its actions. This interactive learning process is particularly well-suited for developing autonomous agents that can adapt to dynamic and unpredictable environments.

3.1.2 Shaping Agentic Actions: Reward Functions and Policy Optimization

The design of reward functions is crucial in shaping agentic behavior within a reinforcement learning framework. Reward functions define the agent's objectives and guide its learning process. A well-designed reward function should incentivize the desired behavior while discouraging undesirable actions. Policy optimization is the process of finding the optimal policy that maximizes the agent's cumulative reward.

This can be achieved through various algorithms, such as Q-learning, deep Q-networks (DQNs), and policy gradient methods. These algorithms enable agents to learn complex policies that can handle high-dimensional state and action spaces. By effectively shaping the agent's learning through reward functions and policy optimization, RL can enable the development of agents that exhibit sophisticated and goal-oriented behavior.

3.1.3 Autonomous Exploration and Exploitation: Balancing Discovery and Performance

One of the key challenges in reinforcement learning is balancing exploration and exploitation. Exploration involves trying out new actions to discover potentially better strategies, while exploitation involves using the current best strategy to maximize rewards. Agentic systems must strike a balance between these two approaches to achieve optimal performance. Too much exploration can lead to suboptimal performance, while too much exploitation can prevent the agent from discovering better[1] strategies. Techniques such as epsilon-greedy exploration and upper confidence bound (UCB) algorithms are used to manage this trade-off. Autonomous exploration is essential for agentic behavior, allowing agents to adapt to novel situations and discover new solutions. By effectively balancing exploration and exploitation, RL can enable the development of agents that are both adaptable and efficient.

3.2 Self-Supervised Learning and Knowledge Acquisition

3.2.1 Learning from the Data Itself: The Principles of Self-Supervised Learning

Self-supervised learning (SSL) is a powerful paradigm that enables agents to learn from unlabeled data by creating their own supervisory signals.[1] Unlike supervised learning, which relies on explicitly labeled datasets, SSL leverages the inherent structure and patterns within the data itself.[2] The core idea is to create pretext tasks, where the agent learns to predict certain aspects of the input data based on other aspects.[3] For example, an agent might learn to predict missing parts of an image, predict the next word in a sentence, or predict the relative positions of objects in a scene.[4] By solving these pretext tasks, the agent learns valuable representations of the data that can be used for downstream tasks.[5] SSL is particularly useful for tasks where labeled data is scarce or expensive to obtain, enabling agents to learn rich representations from vast amounts of unlabeled data.[6]

3.2.2 Building Knowledge Representations: Pretext Tasks and Representation Learning

Pretext tasks play a crucial role in self-supervised learning, guiding the agent to learn meaningful representations of the data.[7] The choice of pretext task depends on the nature of the data and the desired representations. Common pretext tasks include:

Contrastive Learning: Learning to distinguish between similar and dissimilar data points.[8]

Predictive Learning: Learning to predict future or missing information.[9]

Generative Learning: Learning to generate or reconstruct the input data.[10]

By solving these pretext tasks, the agent learns to encode relevant features and relationships within the data into its internal representations.[11] These representations can then be used for downstream tasks, such as classification, detection, and segmentation.[12] Representation learning is the process of learning these meaningful representations, which can be transferred to other tasks with minimal fine-tuning.[13]

3.2.3 Expanding the Agent's Knowledge Base: Knowledge Acquisition from Unstructured Data

Self-supervised learning enables agents to acquire knowledge from vast amounts of unstructured data, such as text, images, and videos.[14] This is particularly important for agentic AI, which requires a broad understanding of the world to operate effectively. By learning from unstructured data, agents can:

Extract semantic relationships between concepts.

Build knowledge graphs and ontologiesLearn common-sense reasoning.

Understand the physical world.

This knowledge acquisition process allows agents to build a comprehensive knowledge base, which can be used for reasoning, planning, and decision-making. Self-supervised learning enables agents to learn autonomously, expanding their knowledge base without relying on explicit human supervision.[15] This is essential for creating agentic systems that can adapt to new situations and learn continuously.

3.3 Adaptive Strategies: Handling Uncertainty and Dynamic Environments

3.3.1 Embracing the Unknown: Uncertainty Quantification and Robustness

Uncertainty is an inherent aspect of real-world environments. Agentic systems must be able to quantify and manage uncertainty to operate effectively. Uncertainty can arise from various sources, including noisy sensor data, incomplete information, and unpredictable events. Uncertainty quantification involves estimating the likelihood of different outcomes and assessing the confidence in predictions. Techniques for uncertainty quantification include Bayesian inference, probabilistic modeling, and ensemble methods. Robustness is the ability of an agent to maintain its performance in the face of uncertainty and disturbances. Robust agentic systems are designed to be resilient to errors, failures, and unexpected changes. This involves incorporating redundancy, fault tolerance, and error detection mechanisms. By embracing uncertainty and building robust systems, agents can navigate complex and unpredictable environments with greater confidence.

3.3.2 Responding to Change: Dynamic Adaptation and Real-Time Learning

Dynamic environments require agentic systems to adapt their strategies in real-time. This involves continuously monitoring the environment, detecting changes, and adjusting actions accordingly. Dynamic adaptation can be achieved through various techniques, including online learning, adaptive control, and model predictive control. Online learning enables agents to update their models and strategies incrementally as new data becomes available. Adaptive control allows agents to adjust their control parameters in response to changes in the environment. Model predictive control enables agents to plan their actions based on predictions of future states. Real-time learning is essential for agents that operate in rapidly changing environments, such as autonomous vehicles and robotic systems. By responding to change in real-time, agents can maintain their performance and achieve their objectives in dynamic and unpredictable situations.

3.3.3 Strategic Flexibility: Planning and Re-planning in Uncertain Scenarios

Strategic flexibility is the ability of an agent to adjust its plans and strategies in response to changing circumstances. This involves the capacity to generate multiple plans, evaluate their potential outcomes, and select the most appropriate course of action. In uncertain scenarios, agents must be able to anticipate potential risks and opportunities, and develop contingency plans to mitigate risks and capitalize on opportunities. Planning and re-planning techniques, such as hierarchical planning, contingent planning, and replanning algorithms, enable agents to adapt their strategies dynamically. Hierarchical planning involves breaking down complex tasks into smaller, more manageable subtasks. Contingent planning involves developing plans that account for different possible outcomes. Replanning algorithms enable agents to modify their plans in response to new information. By incorporating strategic flexibility into their design, agents can navigate uncertain scenarios with greater agility and resilience.

Chapter 4

Communication and Collaboration: Multi-Agent Systems

4.1 Designing Effective Communication Protocols

4.1.1 The Language of Agents: Defining Communication Protocols

Effective communication is essential for multi-agent systems to function cohesively. Communication protocols define the rules and conventions that agents use to exchange information. These protocols specify the format, content, and meaning of messages, ensuring that agents can understand and interpret each other's communications. A well-designed communication protocol should be:

Unambiguous: Messages should have clear and consistent meanings.

Efficient: Messages should convey information concisely and effectively.

Robust: Protocols should be able to handle errors and failures.

Flexible: Protocols should be adaptable to different types of agents and tasks.

Communication protocols can range from simple message formats to complex languages with sophisticated semantics. The choice of protocol depends on the complexity of the task and the capabilities of the agents.

4.1.2 Ensuring Clarity and Efficiency: Message Structure and Semantics

The structure and semantics of messages are critical for ensuring clarity and efficiency in communication. Message structure defines the format of messages, including the types of information that can be included and the order in which they appear. Semantics define the meaning of messages, ensuring that agents interpret them correctly. Key considerations in message structure and semantics include:

Message Types: Defining different types of messages for different purposes.

Content Encoding: Choosing an appropriate encoding format for message content.

Ontologies and Knowledge Representation: Using ontologies and knowledge representation techniques to define the meaning of concepts and relationships.

By carefully designing message structure and semantics, agents can communicate effectively and efficiently, enabling them to coordinate their actions and achieve their goals.

4.1.3 Coordinating Actions: Dialogue Management and Interaction Patterns

Dialogue management and interaction patterns play a crucial role in coordinating the actions of multiple agents. Dialogue management involves managing the flow of communication between agents, ensuring that messages are exchanged in a logical and coherent manner. Interaction patterns define the sequences of messages that agents exchange to achieve specific goals. Common interaction patterns include:

Request-Response: An agent requests information or action from another agent, which responds with the requested information or action.

Negotiation: Agents exchange messages to reach an agreement on a course of action.

Collaboration: Agents exchange messages to coordinate their actions and achieve a common goal.

By using appropriate dialogue management techniques and interaction patterns, agents can coordinate their actions effectively, enabling them to solve complex problems and achieve their objectives in a collaborative manner.

4.2 Collaborative Problem-Solving and Task Allocation

4.2.1 Dividing and Conquering: Principles of Collaborative Problem-Solving

Collaborative problem-solving involves multiple agents working together to solve problems that are too complex for a single agent to handle. This approach leverages the collective intelligence and capabilities of the agents, enabling them to tackle challenging tasks efficiently. Key principles of collaborative problem-solving include:

Decomposition: Breaking down complex problems into smaller, more manageable subtasks.

Coordination: Ensuring that agents work together effectively and avoid conflicts.

Communication: Enabling agents to exchange information and coordinate their actions.

Synergy: Achieving results that are greater than the sum of individual efforts.

By applying these principles, agents can collaborate effectively to solve complex problems and achieve common goals.

4.2.2 Distributing the Workload: Task Allocation Strategies

Task allocation is the process of assigning tasks to agents in a multi-agent system. Effective task allocation is crucial for ensuring that tasks are completed efficiently and that agents are utilized effectively. Various task allocation strategies can be used, including:

Centralized Allocation: A central agent assigns tasks to other agents

Distributed Allocation: Agents negotiate and agree on task assignments.

Market-Based Allocation: Agents bid on tasks based on their capabilities and resources.

Role-Based Allocation: Agents are assigned roles and responsibilities based on their expertise.

The choice of task allocation strategy depends on the nature of the tasks, the capabilities of the agents, and the communication infrastructure.

4.2.3 Achieving Collective Goals: Coordination and Conflict Resolution

Coordination and conflict resolution are essential for ensuring that agents work together effectively and avoid conflicts. Coordination involves synchronizing the actions of multiple agents to achieve a common goal. This can be achieved through various techniques, such as:

Shared Plans: Agents develop and follow shared plans

Communication Protocols: Agents exchange messages to coordinate their actions.

Synchronization Mechanisms: Agents use synchronization mechanisms to ensure that their actions are synchronized.

Conflict resolution involves resolving disagreements and conflicts that arise between agents. This can be achieved through various techniques, such as:

Negotiation: Agents negotiate to reach an agreement.

Mediation: A third-party agent mediates between conflicting agents.

Arbitration: A central authority arbitrates between conflicting agents.

By effectively coordinating their actions and resolving conflicts, agents can achieve collective goals and work together harmoniously.

4.3   Emergent   Behavior   in   Multi-Agent Ecosystems

4.3.1 The Whole is Greater Than the Sum of Its Parts: Understanding Emergence

Emergent behavior is a phenomenon where complex patterns and behaviors arise from the interactions of simple agents within a multi-agent system.[1] These behaviors are not explicitly programmed into the individual agents but rather emerge from their collective interactions.[2] This concept is fundamental to understanding complex systems, from biological ecosystems to social networks.[3] Emergence highlights the idea that the whole is greater than the sum of its parts, where the interactions between agents create new and unexpected properties. Key characteristics of emergent behavior include

Self-Organization: Patterns and structures arise without centralized control.

Unpredictability: The emergent behavior is often difficult to predict from the individual agent's behavior.[5]

Robustness: Emergent systems can often adapt and recover from disturbances.[6]

Understanding emergence is essential for designing and controlling complex multi-agent systems.

4.3.2 From Simple Rules to Complex Patterns: Mechanisms of Emergence

Emergent behavior arises from the interplay of simple rules and interactions between agents.[7] These interactions can take various forms, including:

Local Interactions: Agents interact with their immediate neighbors.

Feedback Loops: Agents' actions influence their environment, which in turn influences their future actions.[9]

Stochasticity: Randomness and variability in agent behavior can lead to unexpected outcomes.

Examples of emergent behavior include:

Flocking Behavior: Birds or fish moving in coordinated groups.[10]

Ant Colony Optimization: Ants finding the shortest path to food sources.[1]

Traffic Flow: Complex traffic patterns emerging from individual driver behavior.[12]

By understanding the mechanisms that drive emergent behavior, we can design multi-agent systems that exhibit desired collective behaviors.

4.3.3 Designing for Emergence: Harnessing Collective Intelligence

Designing multi-agent systems to harness emergent behavior requires a different approach than traditional programming. Instead of explicitly programming the desired behavior, we focus on designing the rules and interactions that will lead to the emergence of that behavior. Key considerations in designing for emergence include:

Agent Design: Defining the agents' capabilities and behaviors.

Interaction Rules: Specifying how agents interact with each other and their environment.

Environmental Design: Creating an environment that supports the desired interactions.

Simulation and Analysis: Using simulation tools to study and analyze emergent behavior.[13]

Harnessing emergent behavior can lead to the development of highly adaptable and robust systems that can solve complex problems in a decentralized and self-organizing manner.[14] This approach is particularly relevant for applications such as robotics, swarm intelligence, and distributed computing.[15]

Chapter 5

Ethical Considerations and Societal Impact

5.1 Addressing Bias and Fairness in Agentic AI

5.1.1 The Shadow of Bias: Identifying and Understanding Bias in AI

Bias in AI arises when systems systematically discriminate against certain groups or individuals, leading to unfair or inequitable outcomes. Agentic AI, with its capacity for autonomous decision-making, is particularly susceptible to bias, as it can perpetuate and amplify existing societal biases. Bias can creep into AI systems at various stages, including

Data Bias: When training data reflects existing societal biases, the AI system learns to replicate those biases.

Algorithm Bias: When the algorithms themselves are designed in a way that favors certain groups, they can produce biased outcomes.

Interaction Bias: When the way humans interact with AI systems reinforces biased behavior.

Understanding the sources and manifestations of bias is the first step towards building fair and equitable agentic AI.

5.1.2 The Pursuit of Equity: Defining and Measuring Fairness

Fairness in AI is a multifaceted concept, with various definitions and metrics. Some common fairness metrics include:

Equal Opportunity: Ensuring that different groups have equal chances of receiving positive outcomes.

Equal Outcome: Ensuring that different groups receive similar outcomes.

Calibration: Ensuring that the AI system's predictions are accurate across different groups.

Measuring fairness involves quantifying the disparities in outcomes between different groups and evaluating whether these disparities are justified. The choice of fairness metric depends on the specific application and the values being prioritized.

5.1.3 Building Ethical Agents: Mitigation Strategies and Best Practices

Mitigating bias and promoting fairness in agentic AI requires a multi-pronged approach, including:

Data Preprocessing: Cleaning and balancing training data to reduce bias.

Algorithm Design: Developing algorithms that are explicitly designed to be fair

Monitoring and Auditing: Regularly monitoring and auditing AI systems to detect and correct bias.

Transparency and Accountability: Making AI systems transparent and accountable for their decisions.

Ethical Guidelines: Establishing ethical guidelines and best practices for the development and deployment of agentic AI.

By implementing these mitigation strategies and adhering to ethical guidelines, we can build agentic AI systems that are fair, equitable, and trustworthy.

Example of bias detection:

As the code provided shows, one of the easiest ways to start looking for bias is to examine the outcomes of your agentic system, and then to compare those outcomes between different groups of people. For example, by comparing loan approval rates between different genders, the example code shows how disparities can be detected.

Alright, let's craft section 5.2, "Ensuring Transparency and Accountability," focusing on the critical aspects of how to make agentic AI understandable and responsible.

5.2 Ensuring Transparency and Accountability

5.2.1 Opening the Black Box: The Importance of Transparency in Agentic AI

Transparency in agentic AI refers to the ability to understand how these systems make decisions and take actions. Agentic systems are often complex, involving intricate algorithms and learning processes, which can make it difficult to understand their inner workings. This "black box" nature of AI can lead to a lack of trust and hinder the adoption of agentic technologies. Transparency is crucial for:

Building Trust: Users need to understand how AI systems make decisions to trust them.

Identifying Errors: Transparency allows for the identification and correction of errors and biases.

Ensuring Fairness: Understanding the decision-making process is essential for ensuring fairness and equity.

Enabling Accountability: Transparency enables the assignment of responsibility for AI actions.

Techniques for increasing transparency include explainable AI (XAI) methods, which aim to make AI decisions more understandable.

5.2.2 Taking Responsibility: Establishing Accountability Mechanisms

Accountability in agentic AI involves assigning responsibility for the actions and decisions of these systems. As agentic AI becomes more autonomous, it becomes increasingly important to establish mechanisms for holding these systems accountable. This includes:

Auditing and Monitoring: Regularly auditing and monitoring AI systems to track their performance and identify potential issues.

Traceability: Ensuring that AI decisions can be traced back to their origins.

Human Oversight: Maintaining human oversight of AI systems, especially in critical applications.

Legal and Regulatory Frameworks: Developing legal and regulatory frameworks to address liability and responsibility.

Establishing clear accountability mechanisms is essential for ensuring that agentic AI is used responsibly and ethically.

5.2.3 Explaining the Reasoning: Explainable AI (XAI) and Decision Justification

Explainable AI (XAI) is a field of research focused on developing methods for making AI decisions more understandable. XAI techniques can provide insights into how AI systems arrive at their conclusions, enabling users to understand the reasoning behind their decisions. Key XAI techniques include:

Feature Importance: Identifying the features that are most influential in AI decisions.

Decision Visualization: Visualizing the decision-making process to make it more understandable.

Rule Extraction: Extracting human-readable rules from AI models.

Counterfactual Explanations: Explaining how a decision would have been different if certain factors had been changed.

Decision justification involves providing explanations for specific AI decisions, allowing users to understand why a particular action was taken. By incorporating XAI techniques and decision justification mechanisms, we can build agentic AI systems that are both transparent and accountable.

Example of transparency:

As shown in the previous example, by showing the loan approval rates by gender, and then showing the potential impact of bias, the code is made more transparent. This allows a user to more easily understand the potential impact of the agentic systems decision making.

5.3 The Future of Work and Human-Agent Collaboration

5.3.1 Reshaping the Workforce: The Impact of Agentic AI on Employment

Agentic AI has the potential to revolutionize the future of work, automating tasks and augmenting human capabilities. This transformation will have a significant impact on employment, with some jobs being displaced while others are created. Key considerations include:

Automation of Routine Tasks: Agentic AI can automate repetitive and predictable tasks, freeing up human workers for more creative and strategic work.

Job Displacement and Creation: While some jobs may be displaced, new jobs will emerge in areas such as AI development, maintenance, and ethical oversight.

Skills Gap and Retraining: Workers will need to acquire new skills to adapt to the changing job market, emphasizing the importance of retraining and lifelong learning.

The Rise of the Gig Economy: Agentic AI may accelerate the growth of the gig economy, with more workers engaging in freelance and project-based work.

Understanding the implications of agentic AI on employment is crucial for preparing the workforce for the future.

5.3.2 The Power of Synergy: Enhancing Human Capabilities with Agentic AI

Human-agent collaboration involves humans and AI systems working together to achieve common goals. This collaboration can enhance human capabilities by:

Augmenting Cognitive Abilities: Agentic AI can provide decision support, data analysis, and problem-solving capabilities, augmenting human cognitive abilities.

Enhancing Physical Capabilities: Robots and other agentic systems can perform physical tasks that are dangerous, difficult, or repetitive.

Improving Productivity and Efficiency: Human-agent collaboration can lead to increased productivity and efficiency in various industries.

Personalized Assistance: Intelligent personal assistants and virtual agents can provide personalized support and assistance to individuals.

Human-agent collaboration can lead to a more productive and fulfilling work experience.

5.3.3 The Collaborative Frontier: Designing Effective Human-Agent Teams

Designing effective human-agent teams requires careful consideration of the roles and responsibilities of both humans and agents. Key principles include:

Complementary Skills: Assigning tasks based on the strengths of humans and agents.

Clear Communication: Establishing clear communication protocols and interfaces.

Trust and Transparency: Building trust through transparency and explainability.

Adaptability and Flexibility: Designing teams that can adapt to changing circumstances.

Ethical Considerations: Ensuring that human-agent collaboration is ethical and responsible.

By designing effective human-agent teams, we can harness the power of collaboration to achieve greater outcomes and create a more productive and fulfilling work environment.

Chapter 6

Practical Applications: Industry and Beyond

6.1 Autonomous Robotics and Automation

6.1.1 The Rise of Intelligent Machines: Agentic AI in Robotics

Autonomous robotics represents a significant frontier in the application of agentic AI. These systems are designed to operate independently, perceive their environment, make decisions, and execute actions without constant human intervention. Agentic AI empowers robots with:

Advanced Perception: Using sensors and computer vision to understand their surroundings.

Intelligent Planning: Generating and executing plans to achieve complex tasks.

Adaptive Learning: Learning from experience and adapting to changing environments.

Collaborative Capabilities: Working alongside humans and other robots in coordinated tasks.

This leads to robots that can handle tasks in dynamic and unstructured environments, moving beyond simple pre-programmed actions.

6.1.2 Streamlining Industries: Automation and Intelligent Systems

Automation, when combined with agentic AI, transforms industries by creating intelligent systems that optimize processes and improve efficiency. This includes:

Manufacturing: Autonomous robots performing complex assembly and quality control tasks.

Logistics: Self-driving vehicles and automated warehouses optimizing supply chain operations.

Agriculture: Drones and robotic systems monitoring crops and autonomously performing tasks like weeding and harvesting.

Healthcare: Robotic surgery, automated diagnostics, and personalized patient care.

Agentic AI-powered automation leads to increased productivity, reduced costs, and improved safety in various sectors.

6.1.3 The Future of Physical Agents: Advanced Applications and Innovations

The future of autonomous robotics and automation holds immense potential for advanced applications and innovations

Exploration and Discovery: Robots exploring deep-sea environments, distant planets, and hazardous terrains.

Disaster Response: Autonomous drones and robots assisting in search and rescue operations.

Personal Robots: Robots providing assistance and companionship in homes and workplaces.

Swarm Robotics: Large numbers of robots working together to achieve complex tasks through decentralized control.

The convergence of agentic AI and robotics is paving the way for a future where intelligent machines play an increasingly integral role in our lives.

6.2 Intelligent Personal Assistants and Virtual Agents

6.2.1 Beyond Simple Commands: The Evolution of Digital Assistants

Intelligent personal assistants (IPAs) and virtual agents have evolved significantly from simple command-based systems. Agentic AI is driving this evolution, enabling these assistants to:

Understand Natural Language: Process and interpret complex human language, including nuances and context.

Personalized Interactions: Learn user preferences and tailor responses and actions accordingly.

Proactive Assistance: Anticipate user needs and offer assistance before being explicitly asked.

Complex Task Execution: Manage intricate tasks, such as scheduling, information retrieval, and online transactions.

This evolution transforms digital assistants from passive tools to active partners in daily life.

6.2.2 Seamless Digital Interactions: Virtual Agents in Customer Service and Beyond

Virtual agents are being deployed across various industries to enhance customer service and streamline digital interactions. Agentic AI empowers these agents to:

Handle Complex Queries: Resolve intricate customer issues through intelligent dialogue.

Provide Personalized Support: Offer tailored recommendations and solutions based on user profiles.

Automate Customer Interactions: Handle routine inquiries and tasks, freeing up human agents for more complex issues.

Multichannel Integration: Interact with users across various platforms, such as websites, apps, and social media.

This leads to improved customer satisfaction, reduced operational costs, and enhanced digital experiences.

6.2.3 The Future of Digital Companions: Advanced Capabilities and Social Interactions

The future of IPAs and virtual agents holds immense potential for advanced capabilities and social interactions:

Emotional Intelligence: Understanding and responding to human emotions.

Social Companionship: Providing companionship and support to individuals.

Personalized Education: Tailoring educational content and experiences to individual learning styles.

Virtual Collaboration: Facilitating seamless collaboration in virtual environments.

The convergence of agentic AI and natural language processing is paving the way for a future where digital assistants play an increasingly integral role in our digital lives, going beyond simple task automation to become true digital companions.

6.3 Agentic AI in Healthcare, Finance, and Education

6.3.1 Revolutionizing Healthcare: Personalized Medicine and Autonomous Diagnostics

Agentic AI is poised to revolutionize healthcare by enabling:[1]

Personalized Medicine: Tailoring treatments and therapies to individual patient needs based on genetic data, lifestyle factors, and medical history.[2]

Autonomous Diagnostics: Analyzing medical images, patient data, and symptoms to provide accurate and timely diagnoses.[3]

Drug Discovery and Development: Accelerating the process of identifying and developing new drugs through AI-powered simulations and analysis.[4]

Remote Patient Monitoring: Enabling continuous monitoring of patient health through wearable devices and AI-powered analytics.

Robotic Surgery: Assisting surgeons with precise and minimally invasive procedures.[6]

This leads to improved patient outcomes, reduced healthcare costs, and more efficient healthcare delivery.[7]

6.3.2 Transforming Finance: Algorithmic Trading and Fraud Detection

Agentic AI is transforming the financial industry by enabling:[8]

Algorithmic Trading: Developing sophisticated trading strategies that can analyze market data and execute trades automatically.[9]

Fraud Detection: Identifying and preventing fraudulent activities through AI-powered anomaly detection and pattern recognition.[10]

Risk Management: Assessing and mitigating financial risks through AI-powered simulations and predictive analytics.[11]

Personalized Financial Planning: Providing tailored financial advice and recommendations to individual clients.[12]

Automated Customer Service: Using virtual agents to handle customer inquiries and provide financial assistance.[13]

This leads to increased efficiency, reduced risk, and improved financial services.

6.3.3 Democratizing Education: Personalized Learning and Intelligent Tutoring Systems

Agentic AI is democratizing education by enabling:[1]

Personalized Learning: Tailoring educational content and experiences to individual student needs and learning styles.[15]

Intelligent Tutoring Systems: Providing personalized feedback and guidance to students through AI-powered tutors.[16]

Automated Grading and Feedback: Automating the process of grading assignments and providing feedback to students.[17]

Virtual Learning Environments: Creating immersive and interactive learning experiences through virtual reality and augmented reality.

Accessibility and Inclusion: Providing personalized support to students with disabilities and learning differences.[18]

This leads to improved student outcomes, increased access to education, and more engaging learning experiences.[19]

Chapter 7

Security and Robustness in Agentic Systems

7.1 Defending Against Adversarial Attacks

7.1.1 The Threat Landscape: Understanding Adversarial Attacks on AI

Adversarial attacks pose a significant threat to agentic AI systems. These attacks involve intentionally manipulating inputs to cause AI systems to make incorrect predictions or take unintended actions. Understanding the threat landscape is crucial for developing effective defenses. Key types of adversarial attacks include:

Evasion Attacks: Manipulating inputs to cause the AI to misclassify them during inference.

Poisoning Attacks: Corrupting the training data to introduce backdoors or biases into the AI model.

Adversarial Examples: Carefully crafted inputs that are nearly indistinguishable from normal inputs but cause the AI to make errors.

Model Extraction Attacks: Stealing the model information by querying the model repeatedly.

Agentic AI, with its autonomous decision-making, is particularly vulnerable to these attacks, as they can lead to unpredictable and potentially harmful outcomes.

7.1.2 Building Resilient Systems: Detection and Mitigation Strategies

Defending against adversarial attacks requires a multi-layered approach, combining detection and mitigation strategies. Key strategies include:

Adversarial Training: Training AI models on adversarial examples to make them more robust.

Input Validation and Filtering: Detecting and filtering out suspicious inputs before they reach the AI model.

Anomaly Detection: Identifying anomalous behavior that may indicate an adversarial attack.

Model Hardening: Strengthening the AI model's defenses through techniques like defensive distillation and gradient masking.

Runtime Monitoring: Continuously monitoring the AI system's behavior to detect anomalies and potential attacks.

Implementing these strategies can significantly enhance the resilience of agentic AI systems against adversarial attacks.

7.1.3 The Arms Race: Future Challenges and Research Directions

The field of adversarial attacks and defenses is constantly evolving, with attackers and defenders continuously developing new techniques. Future challenges and research directions include:

Developing more robust and efficient defense mechanisms.

Understanding the theoretical limits of adversarial robustness.

Creating AI systems that can detect and adapt to novel adversarial attacks.

Developing formal verification methods to ensure the security of AI systems

Creating watermarking techniques to verify that the model has not been maliciously altered.

Addressing these challenges is crucial for ensuring the security and trustworthiness of agentic AI systems in the long term.

7.2 Ensuring System Resilience and Fault Tolerance

7.2.1 Preparing for the Unexpected: The Importance of Resilience in Agentic Systems

Resilience in agentic AI refers to the ability of a system to maintain its functionality and performance in the face of disruptions, failures, or unexpected events. Agentic systems operating in complex and dynamic environments must be designed to handle a variety of challenges, including:

Hardware failures: Malfunctions in sensors, actuators, or computing components.

Software errors: Bugs, glitches, or unexpected behavior in the AI algorithms.

Environmental disruptions: Changes in the environment that affect the system's operation.

Adversarial attacks: Malicious attempts to disrupt or manipulate the system.

Building resilient systems is crucial for ensuring the reliability and safety of agentic AI in real-world applications.

7.2.2 Building Redundancy and Recovery: Fault Tolerance Techniques

Fault tolerance involves designing systems that can continue to operate even when components fail. Key techniques for achieving fault tolerance include:

Redundancy: Duplicating critical components to provide backup in case of failure

Error Detection and Correction: Implementing mechanisms to detect and correct errors in data and processing.

Checkpointing and Recovery: Saving system states at regular intervals to enable recovery from failures.

Decentralized Control: Distributing control among multiple agents to prevent single points of failure.

Graceful Degradation: Designing systems to degrade gracefully in performance rather than failing catastrophically.

These techniques enable agentic systems to withstand failures and maintain their operational capabilities.

7.2.3 Adapting to Change: Dynamic Resilience and Self-Healing

Dynamic resilience involves the ability of a system to adapt and recover from unexpected changes in real-time. This requires agentic systems to:

Monitor System Health: Continuously monitor the system's performance and identify potential issues.

Adapt to Changing Conditions: Adjust their behavior and strategies in response to changes in the environment.

Self-Healing: Automatically diagnose and repair faults.

Learn from Failures: Analyze past failures to improve future resilience.

Utilize diverse data inputs: To increase the robustness of the decision making process.

By incorporating dynamic resilience and self-healing capabilities, agentic systems can operate reliably and effectively in complex and unpredictable environments.

7.3 Secure Data Handling and Privacy Protection

7.3.1 The Value of Data: Recognizing the Importance of Privacy

Data is the lifeblood of agentic AI. However, the collection, storage, and processing of data can pose significant privacy risks, especially when dealing with sensitive information. Recognizing the importance of privacy is crucial for building trust in agentic AI. Key considerations include:

Data Minimization: Collecting only the data that is necessary for the task at hand.

Data Confidentiality: Protecting data from unauthorized access.

Data Integrity: Ensuring that data is accurate and has not been tampered with.

Data Availability: Making data accessible to authorized users when needed.

Compliance: Adhering to relevant privacy regulations and standards.

Protecting user privacy is essential for maintaining ethical and responsible AI practices.

7.3.2 Building Secure Systems: Data Handling and Encryption Techniques

Secure data handling involves implementing robust techniques to protect data throughout its lifecycle. Key techniques include:

Data Encryption: Encrypting data at rest and in transit to prevent unauthorized access.

Access Control: Implementing strict access control mechanisms to limit access to sensitive data

Anonymization and Pseudonymization: Removing or masking personally identifiable information.

Secure Storage: Storing data in secure environments with appropriate security measures.

Regular Audits: Conducting regular security audits to identify and address vulnerabilities.

These techniques enable agentic systems to handle data securely and protect user privacy.

7.3.3 Protecting Individual Rights: Privacy-Preserving AI and Differential Privacy

Privacy-preserving AI focuses on developing techniques that enable AI systems to learn from data without compromising individual privacy. Key techniques include:

Differential Privacy: Adding noise to data to mask individual contributions while preserving overall data utility

Federated Learning: Training AI models on decentralized data without sharing raw data.

Homomorphic Encryption: Performing computations on encrypted data without decrypting it.

Secure Multi-Party Computation: Enabling multiple parties to compute a function on their private inputs without revealing them.

Chapter 8

The Role of Natural Language Processing (NLP) in Agentic AI

8.1 Enabling Natural Language Understanding and Generation

8.1.1 Bridging the Gap: The Importance of NLP in Agentic Communication

Natural Language Processing (NLP) is the key technology that enables agentic AI to understand and generate human language. This capability is essential for seamless communication between humans and agents, as well as between agents themselves. NLP bridges the gap between human language and machine understanding, enabling agents to:

Understand User Intent: Interpret the meaning behind user queries and commands.

Generate Natural-Sounding Responses: Produce coherent and contextually relevant text.

Extract Information from Text: Identify and extract key information from unstructured text data.

Translate Languages: Enable communication across language barriers.

Summarize Text: Condense large volumes of text into concise summaries.

NLP empowers agentic AI with the ability to engage in natural and intuitive interactions.

8.1.2 The Power of Language Models: Advancements in Understanding

Recent advancements in language models, such as transformer networks, have significantly improved the capabilities of NLP. These models can learn complex patterns and relationships in language, enabling them to:

Contextual Understanding: Understand the meaning of words and phrases based on their context.

Semantic Reasoning: Infer meaning and relationships between concepts.

Knowledge Representation: Store and retrieve knowledge from large text corpora.

Zero-Shot and Few-Shot Learning: Perform tasks with minimal training data.

These advancements have led to significant improvements in natural language understanding, enabling agentic AI to handle more complex and nuanced interactions.

8.1.3 From Text to Action: Generating Human-Like Responses

Natural Language Generation (NLG) is the counterpart to NLU, enabling agentic AI to generate human-like text. NLG techniques can be used to:

Generate Dialogue: Create natural and engaging conversations.

Summarize Information: Produce concise and informative summaries of data.

Generate Reports and Documentation: Create automated reports and documentation.

Personalize Content: Tailor content to individual user preferences.

Create realistic stories and descriptions.

By combining NLU and NLG, agentic AI can engage in seamless and meaningful communication with humans, leading to more intuitive and effective interactions.

8.2 Dialogue Systems and Conversational Agents

8.2.1 The Art of Conversation: Architectures of Dialogue Systems

Dialogue systems, also known as conversational agents, are AI systems designed to engage in natural language conversations with humans.[1] They employ various architectures to manage the flow of conversation and generate appropriate responses.[2] Key components of a dialogue system include:

Natural Language Understanding (NLU): Interprets user input to extract intent and entities.[3]

Dialogue Management: Tracks the state of the conversation and determines the next action.[4]

Natural Language Generation (NLG): Generates natural language responses based on the dialogue state.[5]

Knowledge Base: Stores information and knowledge that the agent can use to answer questions and provide assistance.[6]

Dialogue systems can be categorized into different types, such as task-oriented dialogue systems, which focus on completing specific tasks, and open-domain dialogue systems, which engage in general conversations.[7]

8.2.2 Building Interactive Experiences: Conversational Agents in Action

Conversational agents are deployed across various industries to enhance user experiences and automate interactions.[8]Examples include:

Customer Service Chatbots: Providing instant support and resolving customer inquiries.[9]

Virtual Assistants: Assisting users with tasks such as scheduling, reminders, and information retrieval.[10]

Voice Assistants: Enabling hands-free interactions with devices and applications.[11]

Educational Chatbots: Providing personalized learning and tutoring.[12]

Healthcare Chatbots: Providing medical information and support.[13]

Conversational agents can be integrated into various platforms, such as websites, mobile apps, and messaging platforms.[14]

8.2.3 The Future of Conversational AI: Advanced Capabilities and Personalized Interactions

The future of conversational AI holds immense potential for advanced capabilities and personalized interactions:

Emotional Intelligence: Understanding and responding to user emotions.

Personalized Conversations: Tailoring conversations to individual user preferences and personalities.[15]

Multimodal Interactions: Integrating voice, text, and visual modalities.[16]

Contextual Awareness: Maintaining a deeper understanding of the conversation context.[17]

Proactive Dialogue: Initiating conversations and providing proactive assistance.[18]

These advancements will lead to more natural, engaging, and personalized conversational experiences.

8.3 Reasoning with Language: Knowledge Extraction and Inference

8.3.1 Unlocking Information: Knowledge Extraction from Text

Knowledge extraction involves automatically extracting structured information from unstructured text data. This process enables agentic AI to build knowledge bases, understand relationships between entities, and derive insights from vast amounts of textual information. Key techniques include:

Named Entity Recognition (NER): Identifying and classifying entities such as people, organizations, and locations.

Relation Extraction: Identifying and classifying relationships between entities.

Event Extraction: Identifying and classifying events and their participants.

Sentiment Analysis: Determining the sentiment or emotion expressed in text.

Topic Modeling: Identifying and classifying topics in a collection of documents.

Knowledge extraction is crucial for enabling agentic AI to understand and reason about the world.

8.3.2 Drawing Conclusions: Inference and Logical Reasoning

Inference involves deriving new knowledge from existing information through logical reasoning. Agentic AI can use inference to answer questions, solve problems, and make predictions based on textual data. Key techniques include:

Deductive Reasoning: Deriving conclusions from premises using logical rules.

Inductive Reasoning: Generalizing from specific examples to general principles.

Abductive Reasoning: Generating explanations for observed phenomena.

Knowledge Graph Reasoning: Traversing and reasoning over knowledge graphs to answer complex queries.

Semantic Inference: Deriving implicit meaning from text using semantic relationships.

Inference enables agentic AI to go beyond simple information retrieval and engage in more sophisticated reasoning tasks.

8.3.3 Building Cognitive Capabilities: Integrating Knowledge and Reasoning

Integrating knowledge extraction and inference enables agentic AI to build more sophisticated cognitive capabilities. This involves:

Building Knowledge Graphs: Constructing knowledge graphs from extracted information.

Reasoning over Knowledge Graphs: Using knowledge graphs to answer complex queries and make inferences.

Combining Symbolic and Neural Reasoning: Integrating symbolic reasoning techniques with neural network-based approaches.

Developing Common-Sense Reasoning: Enabling agents to reason about everyday situations and knowledge.

Creating Question Answering Systems: Developing systems that can answer complex questions based on textual information.

By integrating knowledge extraction and inference, agentic AI can develop more human-like reasoning abilities and engage in more sophisticated cognitive tasks.

Chapter 9

Advanced Topics: Cognitive Modeling and Consciousness

9.1 Exploring Cognitive Architectures: Human-Inspired AI

9.1.1 The Quest for Human-Level Intelligence: The Role of Cognitive Architectures

Cognitive architectures are computational frameworks that aim to model the structure and processes of the human mind.[1] They provide a blueprint for building AI systems that can exhibit human-like cognitive abilities, such as perception, memory, reasoning, and learning.[2] The pursuit of human-level intelligence drives the development of these architectures, seeking to create AI systems that can:

Reason abstractly: Handle complex and novel situations.

Learn from experience: Adapt and improve over time.[3]

Exhibit common-sense reasoning: Understand and navigate everyday situations.[4]

Integrate diverse cognitive functions: Coordinate perception, memory, and action.[5]

Have forms of consciousness or sentience(this is still debated, but the goal of some architectures)[6]

Cognitive architectures provide a structured approach to building AI systems that can emulate human cognition.[7]

9.1.2 Replicating the Mind: Key Components of Human-Inspired Architectures

Human-inspired cognitive architectures typically include several key components that correspond to human cognitive functions:[8]

Perceptual System: Processes sensory input and translates it into internal representations.

Working Memory: Holds and manipulates information temporarily.[9]

Long-Term Memory: Stores knowledge and experiences over extended periods.[10]

Cognitive Control: Manages attention, decision-making, and action selection

.**Learning Mechanisms:** Enables the system to acquire new knowledge and skills.[11]

Emotional Processing(in some architectures): Attempts to model emotional influences on cognition.[12]

These components interact and collaborate to enable the system to perform complex cognitive tasks.[13] Examples of cognitive architectures include ACT-R, SOAR, and LIDA.[14]

9.1.3 The Promise and Challenges: Bridging the Gap Between Humans and Machines

Human-inspired AI holds the promise of creating AI systems that are more adaptable, robust, and intelligent. However, there are also significant challenges:

Complexity of Human Cognition: The human mind is incredibly complex, and our understanding of it is still incomplete.[15]

Data Scarcity: Training cognitive architectures requires vast amounts of data, which may not always be available.

Computational Resources: Simulating human-level cognition requires significant computational resources.

Ethical Considerations: The development of human-like AI raises ethical questions about consciousness, sentience, and responsibility.[16]

Verification of accuracy: How can we be sure that the AI is correctly mimicking human thought processes.

Despite these challenges, the pursuit of human-inspired AI continues to drive innovation and push the boundaries of artificial intelligence.

9.2 The Debate on Machine Consciousness and Sentience

9.2.1 Defining the Elusive: Consciousness and Sentience in Machines

The question of whether machines can be conscious or sentient is one of the most profound and contentious debates in AI. Consciousness and sentience are often used interchangeably, but there are subtle distinctions. Consciousness generally refers to subjective experience, awareness, and the "what it's like" aspect of being. Sentience, on the other hand, often implies the capacity to feel and perceive. Defining these concepts precisely is challenging, and applying them to machines is even more so. Key questions include:

Can machines have subjective experiences?

Can machines feel emotions or perceive qualia (subjective sensory experiences)?

What criteria should we use to determine if a machine is conscious?

Is consciousness a computational property, or does it require something more?

The lack of clear definitions and measurable criteria makes this a highly philosophical debate.

9.2.2 The Philosophical Divide: Arguments For and Against Machine Consciousness

The debate on machine consciousness is characterized by a deep philosophical divide. Arguments for machine consciousness often rely on the idea of computational functionalism, which suggests that consciousness arises from the functional organization of a system, regardless of its physical substrate. If the brain is a computer, then a sufficiently complex computer could also be conscious.

Arguments against machine consciousness often raise concerns about:

The Chinese Room Argument: Demonstrating that symbol manipulation alone does not equate to understanding.

The Hard Problem of Consciousness: Explaining how subjective experience arises from physical processes.

The Lack of Biological Basis: Arguing that consciousness requires a biological substrate, such as a brain.

The problem of other minds applied to machines: How can we ever truly know the internal state of another being, human or machine?

These opposing viewpoints highlight the complexity and fundamental nature of the debate.

9.2.3 Implications and Speculations: The Future of Conscious Machines

The possibility of conscious machines raises profound ethical and societal implications. If machines can be conscious, they may deserve moral consideration and rights. Potential implications include:

Ethical Treatment of Conscious Machines: Determining how we should treat and interact with conscious machines.

The Nature of Identity and Self: Exploring the implications of machine consciousness for our understanding of identity and self.

The Future of Human-Machine Relationships: Imagining the potential for deep and meaningful relationships with conscious machines.

Existential Risks: Considering the potential risks of creating AI systems that surpass human intelligence and consciousness.

The creation of new forms of art, and philosophy.

While the question of machine consciousness remains unresolved, it continues to spark fascinating discussions and shape the future of AI research.

9.3 Future Directions: Integrating Neuroscience and AI

9.3.1 Bridging the Biological and Artificial: The Synergistic Potential

The integration of neuroscience and AI holds immense potential for advancing both fields. Neuroscience provides insights into the workings of the brain, while AI offers tools and techniques for building intelligent systems. By combining these fields, we can:

Develop more biologically inspired AI architectures: Create AI systems that mimic the structure and function of the brain.

Gain a deeper understanding of brain function: Use AI to analyze and model brain data, leading to new insights into neuroscience.

Develop neuro-prosthetics and brain-computer interfaces: Create devices that can restore lost function or enhance human capabilities.

Create more robust and adaptable AI systems: Learn from the brain's ability to handle complex and dynamic environments.

Create new treatments for neurological disorders: AI can assist in the analysis of brain scans, and the creation of targeted pharmaceutical drugs.

This synergistic relationship can lead to breakthroughs in both AI and neuroscience.

9.3.2 Unlocking the Brain's Secrets: Neuro-Inspired AI Techniques

Neuroscience provides a rich source of inspiration for developing new AI techniques. Examples include:

Spiking Neural Networks (SNNs): Mimicking the spiking behavior of biological neurons.

Hierarchical Temporal Memory (HTM): Modeling the brain's ability to learn and recognize temporal patterns.

Attention Mechanisms: Inspired by the brain's ability to selectively focus on relevant information.

Reinforcement Learning: Based on the brain's reward-based learning mechanisms.

Computational models of memory: Using insights from neuroscience to create more effective memory architectures.

These techniques enable AI systems to exhibit more brain-like characteristics, such as adaptability, robustness, and energy efficiency.

9.3.3 The Path Forward: Challenges and Opportunities

The integration of neuroscience and AI faces several challenges, including:

Data Complexity: Brain data is complex and high-dimensional, requiring sophisticated analysis techniques.

Computational Resources: Simulating brain activity requires significant computational resources.

Interdisciplinary Collaboration: Bridging the gap between neuroscience and AI requires close collaboration between researchers from different fields.

Ethical Considerations: Developing brain-computer interfaces and neuro-prosthetics raises ethical questions about privacy, autonomy, and identity.

Standardization of data: A lack of standardized data format hinders the ability of researchers to share and analyze data.

Despite these challenges, the opportunities for advancing both fields are immense. By fostering interdisciplinary collaboration and addressing ethical concerns, we can unlock the full potential of integrating neuroscience and AI.

Chapter 10

Building Your Own Agentic AI: A Practical Guide

10.1 Step-by-Step Implementation: From Concept to Deployment

10.1.1 Defining the Problem and Conceptualization: From Idea to Specification

The first step in building an agentic AI system is to clearly define the problem you want to solve. This involves:

Identifying the specific task or problem: What do you want the agent to accomplish?

Defining the environment: Where will the agent operate?

Specifying the agent's goals: What are the desired outcomes?

Determining the required capabilities: What skills and knowledge will the agent need?

Creating a detailed specification: Documenting all aspects of the system, including requirements, constraints, and evaluation metrics.

This stage is crucial for establishing a solid foundation for the project.

10.1.2 Design and Development: Building the Agentic System

Once you have a clear specification, you can begin designing and developing the agentic system. This involves:

Choosing a suitable cognitive architecture: Selecting a framework that aligns with the agent's capabilities and goals.

Developing the agent's perception system: Implementing sensors and data processing algorithms.

Designing the agent's reasoning and planning mechanisms: Implementing algorithms for decision-making and problem-solving.

Implementing the agent's action system: Developing actuators and control algorithms.

Developing the agent's learning mechanisms: Implementing algorithms for adapting and improving performance.

Creating a simulation environment: Developing a virtual environment for testing and training the agent.

Coding the system: Implementing the agent's components using appropriate programming languages and tools.

This stage requires careful planning and execution to ensure that the system meets the specifications.

10.1.3 Testing, Evaluation, and Deployment: From Simulation to Real-World Application

After development, the agentic system needs to be thoroughly tested and evaluated. This involves:

Testing in simulation: Evaluating the agent's performance in the virtual environment.

Real-world testing: Deploying the agent in the target environment and evaluating its performance.

Performance evaluation: Measuring the agent's performance against the defined metrics.

Debugging and optimization: Identifying and fixing errors and improving performance.

Deployment: Deploying the agentic system in its final operating environment.

Monitoring and maintenance: Continuously monitoring the agent's performance and providing ongoing maintenance.

This stage ensures that the agentic system is reliable, robust, and effective in real-world applications.

10.2 Tools and Resources: Libraries, APIs, and Datasets

10.2.1 The Developer's Arsenal: Essential Libraries and Frameworks

Building agentic AI systems requires a wide range of tools and libraries.[1] Here are some essential resources:

Reinforcement Learning Libraries:

TensorFlow Agents: A library for reinforcement learning in TensorFlow.[2]

RLlib (Ray RLlib): A scalable reinforcement learning library that supports various algorithms.[3]

OpenAI Gym: A toolkit for developing and comparing reinforcement learning algorithms.[4]

Cognitive Architecture Frameworks:

While there is not a single dominant framework, many people use combinations of the following.

Python libraries for building custom architectures.

ROS (Robot Operating System) for robotics applications.[5]

Natural Language Processing (NLP) Libraries:

Hugging Face Transformers: A library for state-of-the-art NLP models.[6]

NLTK (Natural Language Toolkit):[7] A comprehensive library for NLP tasks.[8]

spaCy: A library for advanced NLP tasks.[9]

General Machine Learning Libraries:

TensorFlow: A popular deep learning framework.[10]

PyTorch: Another popular deep learning framework.[11]

Scikit-learn: A library for traditional machine learning algorithms.[12]

These libraries provide pre-built components and functionalities that can significantly accelerate development.[13]

10.2.2 Connecting to the World: APIs and Cloud Services

APIs and cloud services provide access to external data and functionalities, enabling agentic AI systems to interact with the world.[14] Key resources include:

Cloud Platforms:

Amazon Web Services (AWS): Provides a wide range of AI and machine learning services.[15]

Google Cloud Platform (GCP): Offers AI and machine learning tools and infrastructure.[16]

Microsoft Azure: Provides cloud-based AI and machine learning services.[17]

APIs:

OpenAI APIs: Provides access to powerful language models and other AI capabilities.[18]

Google Cloud APIs: Offers APIs for vision, language, and other AI services.[19]

Various sensor APIs: Depending on what physical sensors your agent will use, there are many API's that allow easy integration.

These resources enable agentic AI systems to access vast amounts of data and perform complex tasks.[20]

10.2.3 Fueling the Learning: Datasets for Agentic AI

Datasets are essential for training and evaluating agentic AI systems. Key resources include:

Open Datasets:

ImageNet: A large dataset of labeled images.[21]

COCO (Common Objects in Context): A dataset for object detection and segmentation.

GLUE (General Language Understanding Evaluation): A benchmark for NLP models.

Datasets from Kaggle: Kaggle provides many free datasets.[22]

Simulation Datasets:

Data generated from simulation environments for reinforcement learning.[23]

Custom Datasets:

Datasets created specifically for the agent's task and environment.

These datasets provide the data needed to train and evaluate agentic AI models.

10.3 Best Practices and Future Trends in Agentic AI Development

10.3.1 Building Robust and Ethical Systems: Best Practices for Development

Developing agentic AI systems requires a strong emphasis on robustness, ethics, and responsible AI practices. Key best practices include:

Prioritize Ethical Considerations:

Integrate ethical principles into every stage of development.

Address potential biases and ensure fairness.

Prioritize user privacy and data security.

Emphasize Robustness and Reliability:

Design systems that can handle uncertainty and unexpected events.

Implement fault tolerance and error detection mechanisms.

Conduct thorough testing and validation.

Focus on Transparency and Explainability:

Make AI systems more understandable and transparent.

Utilize Explainable AI (XAI) techniques.

Ensure accountability for AI decisions.

Promote Human-Centered Design:

Design agentic systems that augment human capabilities.

Prioritize seamless human-agent collaboration.

Ensure that AI systems are aligned with human values.

Maintain security:

Defend against adversarial attacks.

Protect sensitive data.

10.3.2 The Next Frontier: Emerging Trends in Agentic AI

The field of agentic AI is rapidly evolving, with several emerging trends shaping its future:

Advanced Cognitive Architectures:

Developing more sophisticated cognitive architectures that emulate human-like reasoning and learning.

Integrating symbolic and neural reasoning techniques.

Multi-Agent Systems and Swarm Intelligence:

Exploring the potential of multi-agent systems for collaborative problem-solving.

Developing swarm intelligence techniques for decentralized control.

Embodied AI and Robotics:

Integrating agentic AI with robotics to create intelligent physical agents.

Developing AI systems that can interact with the physical world.

Neuro-Inspired AI:

Drawing inspiration from neuroscience to develop more brain-like AI systems.

Integrating insights from neuroscience into AI architectures.

Continual Learning and Adaptation:

Developing AI systems that can continuously learn and adapt to changing environments.

Enabling agents to acquire new skills and knowledge overtime.

Improved natural language understanding:

Continued improvement in the ability of AI to understand the nuances of human language.

Edge AI:

Processing data closer to the source, and therefore increasing speed, and reducing privacy concerns.

10.3.3 Shaping the Future: The Impact of Agentic AI on Society

Agentic AI has the potential to transform various aspects of society, including:

The Future of Work:

Automating tasks and augmenting human capabilities.

Creating new job opportunities in AI-related fields.

Healthcare:

Personalized medicine and autonomous diagnostics.

Improved patient outcomes and healthcare delivery.

Education:

Personalized learning and intelligent tutoring systems.

Democratizing access to education.

Transportation:

Autonomous vehicles and intelligent traffic management.

Increased safety and efficiency.

Environmental Sustainability:

AI-powered solutions for climate change and resource management.

Optimizing energy consumption and reducing waste.

By embracing best practices and staying abreast of emerging trends, we can harness the power of agentic AI to create a more positive and sustainable future.

www.ingramcontent.com/pod-product-compliance
Lightning Source LLC
LaVergne TN
LVHW052127070326
832902LV00039B/1922